ANIMALS AT RISK
Tigers In Danger

BY MICHAEL PORTMAN

Gareth Stevens
Publishing

MEET THE TIGER

Tigers are the largest cat **species** in the world. Their strength and beauty have made them both loved and feared. Different kinds of tigers live in different **habitats**, some cold and snowy, and others hot and rainy. However, all tigers like to be in forested areas.

In spite of their powerful build, tigers face serious **threats**. Today, there may be as few as 3,200 tigers living in the wild. If people don't act, tigers may become **extinct**.

Siberian tiger ▶

▼ Tigers are one of the few cats
that enjoy swimming.

Just 100 years ago, there were nine types, or subspecies, of tigers. Today, only six subspecies are left. Siberian, or Amur, tigers are the largest tigers. They mostly live in the forests of eastern Russia, though some have been found in China and North Korea. Bengal, or Indian, tigers are the most common type. India has the largest population. The Indochinese, Malayan, South China, and Sumatran tigers live in several Asian countries. Sadly, all six tiger subspecies are **endangered** because of **poaching** and habitat loss.

baby Sumatran tiger ▶

WILD FACTS

The smallest tiger is the Sumatran. Most adult males are about 8 feet (2.4 m) long and weigh about 220 pounds (100 kg).

An adult male Siberian tiger may be more than 10 feet (3 m) long and weigh more than 650 pounds (295 kg).

Tigers are carnivores, which means they only eat meat. They hunt many sorts of animals, including turtles, frogs, deer, pigs, and even baby elephants. Tigers are usually nocturnal, which means they sleep during the day and hunt at night. They have excellent eyesight and can see well in the dark. Tigers' stripes act as **camouflage**, making it hard for other animals to spot them.

Tigers spend most of their time alone in their own territory. However, they sometimes share a large meal with other tigers.

WILD FACTS

A tiger covers any leftover meat with leaves and dirt. When it's hungry again, it comes back to feed.

 An adult tiger can eat up to 60 pounds (27 kg) of meat a day.

A healthy tiger population depends on the tigers' habitat. Tigers need large amounts of food in order to **survive**. A forest that has a lot of animals is a good habitat because each tiger is able to find plenty of food. However, a forest habitat that has few animals cannot support a large tiger population.

In Russian forests, where there are few animals, tigers have large territories because they must travel long distances in search of food. In India, where there are many animals, a tiger's territory is often much smaller.

WILD FACTS
A tiger's roar can be heard as far as 2 miles (3.2 km) away.

A male tiger protects his territory from other males but may share it with female tigers.

Many tigers live close to people. This has caused problems for both people and tigers. Large areas of tigers' forest habitats have been cleared for lumber and to make room for homes and farms. Tigers that once had large territories must now live in much smaller areas.

People also hunt many of the same animals that tigers eat. Without enough food, hungry tigers attack farm animals instead of their usual **prey**. Because of this, farmers often shoot or poison tigers to keep their livestock safe.

WILD FACTS

Not all tigers are orange and black. Some are black and tan, white and tan, or all white.

In the last 10 years, tigers have lost about 40 percent of their natural habitat.

13

For centuries, people have hunted tigers. Killing a tiger was a sign of bravery. Many people value tiger meat, skin, bones, and other body parts as well.

In China, tiger bones have been used in **medicines** for more than 1,000 years. Tiger skins are used for clothing and decorations. Claws, teeth, and whiskers are sometimes used as good-luck charms.

In recent years, there are so few tigers left in China that Bengal tigers are hunted in India so that they can be sold in China. Although these activities are illegal, poaching continues.

▼ The long front teeth on a tiger are called the canine teeth. They can *be* 3 inches (7.6 cm) long in some species!

SAVE THE MOTHER, SAVE THE CUBS

When a poacher kills a tiger, the loss may be more than just one animal. If a female tiger, or tigress, is raising cubs, killing her may result in the death of the entire family. Female tigers have 2 or 3 cubs every 2 years. The cubs usually can't survive on their own until they're about 2 years old. Cubs younger than this can die from lack of food. Tiger cubs left unguarded can also become prey for other animals, even other tigers.

WILD FACTS
Tigers can live to be more than 20 years old in zoos but usually only live about 15 years in the wild.

Mother tigers raise their cubs alone. Fathers leave before the cubs are born. ▼

To save wild tigers, their forest and jungle habitats throughout Asia must be protected. Tigers must also be protected from poachers. Since the 1990s, the number of tigers killed by poachers has increased.

Today, governments and wildlife groups are working together to solve these problems. **Nature reserves** have been created to keep tigers safe. Governments are also working hard to stop the illegal trade of tiger parts. However, more reserves need to be built and stronger laws against poaching must be put into effect.

WILD FACTS

Tigers raised in zoos usually cannot be freed into the wild. They don't have the skills to survive on their own.

Without a supply of food and clean water, tigers cannot survive.

THE FUTURE OF TIGERS

The **estimated** numbers of wild tigers remaining are very low. However, scientists and wildlife groups think it's possible to double the number of wild tigers over the next 10 years. They named the year 2022 as their goal year. This is the next "Year of the Tiger" in the Chinese calendar. Several countries with tiger habitats, including Russia, India, and China, have agreed to projects to make this population growth possible. Hopefully, 2022 will be the Year of the Tiger in more ways than one.

Estimated Numbers of Tigers in the Wild

Bengal	1,850
Siberian	450
Indochinese	350
Malayan	500
Sumatran	400
South China	not sighted in the wild for 25 years

GLOSSARY

camouflage: a color or pattern that matches surroundings and helps an animal hide

endangered: in danger of dying out

estimated: describing a guess based on knowledge or facts

extinct: having no living members

habitat: an area where plants, animals, and other living things live

medicine: a drug used to treat an illness

nature reserve: a safe area for endangered animals

poaching: illegal hunting

prey: an animal that is hunted by another animal for food

species: a group of animals that are all of the same kind

survive: to stay alive

threat: something likely to cause harm

FOR MORE INFORMATION

BOOKS

Eason, Sarah. *Save the Tiger.* New York, NY: PowerKids Press, 2009.

Jenkins, Martin. *Can We Save the Tiger?* Somerville, MA: Candlewick Press, 2011.

Nobleman, Marc Tyler. *Tigers.* New York, NY: Marshall Cavendish Benchmark, 2009.

WEBSITES

Tiger
www.worldwildlife.org/species/finder/tigers/
Read facts about several subspecies of tigers.

Tigers
kids.nationalgeographic.com/kids/animals/creaturefeature/tiger/
Watch videos, hear sounds, and see pictures of tigers.

INDEX